THE FOUR TYPES OF DOGS
every business needs

How To Build the Right Team To Grow Your Business and Have A Balanced Life

BELLA VASTA

Copyright © 2018 by Bella Vasta

All rights reserved. No part of this publication may be reproduced, distributed, or transmitted in any form or by any means, including photocopying, recording, or other electronic or mechanical methods, without the prior written permission of the publisher, except in the case of brief quotations embodied in critical reviews and certain other noncommercial uses permitted by copyright law.

DEDICATION

I dedicate this book to my loving husband who has been my biggest believer and cheerleader of anything I have ever wanted to do. I also want to thank my incredible daughter for teaching me more about life, miracles, and faith than I ever thought possible. I am grateful to my mother for her endless, loving support, and my dad for planting the seed years ago by telling me I should write a book. Oh, and for giving me a curfew in college! ;)

CONTENTS

Preface	vii
Introduction	ix
1. **Olivia**	1
2. **Pit Bulls: Your Protectors**	5
Lawyers and Insurance Brokers are Our Pit Bulls	6
Case Study - Aubrey	8
Case Study - Char	11
Case Study - Sam	14
Homework	18
3. **The Border Collie: Systems and Processes**	19
Why You Need Border Collies	20
Case Study - Hotel Branding	21
Case Study - Mary Jo	22
Homework	27
4. **Poodle: Numbers and Analytics**	29
Why do we need poodles in our business?	30
Case Study - The Old Bella	34
Case Study - Erica Godwin, The Barketing Blog	36
Homework	40
5. **Jack Russell Terrier: Marketing and Promotions**	41
Why You Need A Jack Russell	42
Case Study - Susan	43
Homework	50
6. **Being A Business Owner is Tough!**	51
7. **Take the Quiz: Which Dog Are You?**	57
Resources	61
About the Author	63

PREFACE

I didn't plan on starting either of the two businesses that I have grown over the past fifteen years. Both started completely by accident. My pet sitting company began as a way to get out of my parents' house while going to college. The curfew they imposed on me in my junior year wasn't to my liking, so I jumped at the chance to get paid $25 a day to dog sit two white dogs for a lady who traveled for work.

Two white fluffy dogs—that is just what they were to me at the time. I was different than the rest of the pet sitters out there. I didn't start the business because I had a love for dogs, rather it was a way to gain independence and make money. Eventually, however, I came to love and understand dogs.

I ran that business for fourteen years before I sold it for six figures. I never dreamt of owning a pet-sitting business, and I never knew I would be a business consultant. When I was little, I wanted to be a waitress because they were always running around. Those were the innocent days when I would play house with the neighborhood girls. We would each claim which New Kids on the Block member was our "husband" and pretend we were married, had babies, and lived happily ever after.

Little did I know, that isn't always the way it goes.

During the twelfth year of that pet-sitting company, in 2014, my husband, Alex, and I were blessed with a child, Olivia. Although it wasn't a normal pregnancy, and she was born as one of the fifty smallest surviving female babies on the planet at only twelve ounces. I continued to run my pet-sitting company and coaching company as I traveled to and from the Neonatal Intensive Care Unit (NICU), barely holding it together. After six months of fighting for her life, Olivia came home. Then the real battles began. Along with learning to cope with eighty hours of nursing care in my home, I had to process what had happened, overcome post traumatic stress disorder, anxiety, and postpartum depression.

Through all the storms that life threw at me, both of my businesses not only survived but thrived while still allowing me to be available for my family's needs and my own. In this book, I will share with you how I was able to navigate a business during times of personal crisis so that you and your business can thrive when life suddenly overwhelms or knocks you down.

INTRODUCTION

Have you ever been to the dog park? Typically, it is a big, open outdoor space with lots of chaos! Dogs are running everywhere. Sometimes their people are engaging with them. Sometimes the dogs want nothing to do with their humans. Depending on the time of day there could be lots of dogs playing together or off separately. Though the purpose of a dog park is for them to get together and run off their energy, not all dogs play together.

Sometimes you will see the chase dogs running circles around the perimeter. It seems like they never get exhausted. Then you have the dogs that are often staying close to their owners like a loyal protector. You might also see some antagonizing others, while some will just keep running and fetching the ball that their parent is throwing rhythmically with the Chuckit!

Whatever it is they are doing, most are fixated on doing something. They are all different, yet (mostly) it all works with them sharing one enclosed area. It creates the dog park. They run as a pack. Without the dogs, the park wouldn't exist, and the pack wouldn't be together. Without the different dogs naturally attracted to doing different things, the concept of the dog park wouldn't work.

Imagine every dog in the park all fetching that one ball? They would fight over it. Or the ones running the perimeter? Usually there is one leading the formation as they go around and around, then split across the park and then back again. Alternatively, if all the dogs were just standing around there wouldn't be much use for the dog park, would there be? The dog park is a place they can all come together, be themselves, and have fun. Some find enjoyment out of the chasing after the ball. Others enjoy just sniffing around and staying near their human, while others need the physical stimulation of running around and around.

Although some believe that the pack mentality has been disproved from a training philosophy standpoint, I would like to loosely use it as a metaphor for this book. Within the chaos of a dog park, you will start to see different packs of dogs form together as groups as they play, sniff, run and chase each other. The point of these groups of dogs coming together is that they are all different, yet together they are able to play together with one another. They get along and enjoy the larger goal of coming together to enjoy the park while co-existing with one another. Simply put, they play well together.

I wanted to write this book for you, the entrepreneur to really help you reframe the "WHY" you are growing your business. As I consult with business owners all around the world, I hear horror stories that include illness, loved ones with cancer, the sudden death of a spouse or child, that their parents are near the end of their lives and they want to fly out of state to be with them during their last weeks. When they tell me these things, it simply breaks my heart because there is also desperation that they are afraid to go because their clients need them. In my mind, I am screaming, "Go! Family is everything! Your health is everything! You shouldn't have to take your work and be accepting client calls while sitting with a loved one during chemotherapy treatments or on your parents' death beds." I hope that you add to your "WHY" for growing your business the goal of being able to afford the choices in life that matter the most.

Building a strong team will enable you to make those choices.

Some business owners try their hardest to do it all on their own or build their team that, despite their best efforts, never seems to click. By helping you solve these issues, you will be able to unlock the freedom to have choices in life. Those are choices that enable you to be with that loved one or take a step back for your own personal reasons. I can guarantee that if you own a business right now, you didn't say when you started it, "Gee. I think I will start a business that takes away all my free time, takes me away from friends and family, jeopardizes my health, and stresses me out." I am willing to bet that you started your business to have those freedom of choices in your life.

Over the years of caring for pets in my former pet sitting company I have come to know that certain breeds have some similar characteristics. You learn that each breed has certain strengths that owners look for when getting their breed specific dog. This team that you will build will do the same. You will be seeking certain characteristics in each dog you attract to your team so you can build your business so strong that you are able to afford a peaceful balance between work and family.

I am going to show you how to seek out and recruit the four vastly different breeds of dogs, as they relate to each other, to keep your business running. You will probably see yourself in one or two of them. It is my hope that by the end of this book you will be able to easily identify which dog you are so you can get to work on building your team by adding those dogs that will do the tasks you struggle with. The self quiz at the end of the book will help you with this as well. When you have all of these breeds on your team, you should have a business that can run without you in it.

That, my friends, is freedom to choose! I want you all to experience this freedom through having your team built and in place, with the proper dogs before you ever need it.

1

OLIVIA

It was Memorial Day 2014. I was five months pregnant, barely even showing. I was sitting in the parking lot about to go into prenatal yoga when my doctor called. "I just received your blood pressure report," she said. "I am calling the hospital and reserving you a bed. I want you to go there now."

Almost in shock, I drove home. I called my husband and told him that we needed to go to the hospital immediately. Then I called my parents. The next thing I knew I was on a gurney in the antepartum wing of the hospital, where a nurse, Kelly, was sticking an IV into my hand (it hurt bad!) and asking me questions as if nothing was wrong at all. I will never forget how calming and nurturing she was to me.

I looked towards the foot of my bed and saw my mom, my dad, and my husband (who all should have been at work) staring back at me looking very concerned. I remember thinking, "Woah. This must be really serious if they are all here for me right now." All of a sudden, I started to feel really light headed, and I was told that the IV was working...

Five days later I was released with the knowledge that my baby wasn't growing inside of me. She probably would not survive they saidty. I was in shock. I was shattered. Needless to say, I didn't want to do anything that pertained to my pet sitting business. That was the last thing I wanted to think about, and my patience grew short with the tasks that needed to be managed.

Thankfully, I was not doing the actual pet sitting, dog walking visits, or the consultations. I had built the business to a point where I had staff being deployed to our client's homes. Ann, my part-time office manager, without even asking, stepped right up and did what was needed to keep the company going. I was so lucky to have her, and I don't know what I would have done had I not had her in place. In fact, if I didn't have her, or my staff, I know for sure my business wouldn't have survived. It is one of the biggest lessons I learned—the difference between a job and a business. A business can run without you involved in it.

I was not in a place where I could absorb the emotions or react professionally to any of pet sitting clients getting upset because a litter box wasn't scooped to their satisfaction or dealing with an emergency that an employee would want me to solve at the last minute. I just didn't have the bandwidth. Honestly, I didn't care about the business at the time because all I could think about was my baby. I was on bed rest, told to keep the stress out of my life, and I just couldn't do what I used to. Luckily, leading up to all of this, I was a stickler for systems and processes. I had developed clear cut processes for the way staff would communicate with the office, the way the clients would communicate with the staff and the office, the way payroll would be run, key inventory, and scheduling. The processes were written down, making it easy for Ann to handle the clients' questions as well as selling to potential new clients who would call in. She was able to look up the information on how to manage the staff, keep the schedule moving, keep the credit cards charging, and the overall operations running. She was successful because I had all of the systems already established.

For twelve years I had been in building mode with the business. When the crisis occurred, I gladly put everything on autopilot. Where, before, I was working on building, now my focus shifted to maintaining. I had all my clients booking 100% online rather than the phone, so it was less work for my office manager and me. I had the staff putting their availability in online, so my scheduling software could do its job. I processed my credit cards on Sunday mornings in bulk taking less than ten minutes. I had strict protocols for everything.

Having these strict protocols enabled me to handle business on my twenty-minute drive to and from the hospital for Olivia's 183 day stay. I called it my "fact mode" where I would talk to my office manager only wanting facts, no explanations. I can't imagine how difficult it was to deal with me during those moments.

The Sale.

My goal had always been to grow the business in my twenties, and, when I finally found Mr. Right, settled down, and started a family, I would sell it. About a year and a half after we took Olivia home from the hospital, I decided it was time to put the business on the market.

I interviewed five brokers. It was important that I interviewed many people. In the end, I picked the broker who said he would have it sold in thirty days for close to the asking price. I thought he was crazy, but he also owned a brokerage that sold "mom and pop businesses" to moms and pops.

Would you believe that in fourteen days he had a letter of intent for me?

I was shocked and really excited. I knew that the company's numbers were good, and that was what was ultimately appealing to the buyer. The person investing knew they could make their money back in a reasonable time. They saw that the business was growing up, up, and up—even despite the trying years I had experienced.

I had proof of concept.

My business selling so quickly for the amount of money I wanted would never have happened without my building a team with the right dogs all playing together. This is something that every business owner needs to learn how to do. Without the ability to choose the proper people to create a winning team, a business's growth will be stunted.

There is no way a business owner can possibly wear all the hats of the team members they need. The four areas every business owner needs to address are protections, systems, numbers, and marketing. Almost everything a business needs can fall into one of these four categories. Understand that the examples I am about to show you are not just limited to the types of people that I describe, but that there are many more types of people you can add to your team that might fit into these categories, and some might even overlap.

2

PIT BULLS: YOUR PROTECTORS

The first people I hired were the pit bulls. "Pit bull" is actually a shorter term referring to the American pit bull terrier, the American Staffordshire terrier, the American Bully, and the Staffordshire Bull terrier. They are loyal, clown-like dogs who love to be active with their human companions. They have been known to be like "bulls in a china cabinet" and, as such, they need to be stimulated mentally and physically. Pit bulls are smart, and I would even say emotional.

Typically, the term "pit bull" strikes fear in people, as they have earned a bad reputation.

They are known as being fighting dogs, vicious, and causing fights and attacks. They are often banned from apartment complexes, and some people walk on the other side of the street when they see one coming.

But that is just the thing, people fear the stereotype and in real life they are loyal and smart.

Peaches & Rufus

Peaches, God rest her soul, was the most loving pit bull my company ever cared for. You could carry this dog in your arms. She had over 10,000 followers on Facebook and was the size of a four-year-old human "baby." She liked to sleep under the covers with her pet sitter at night and would always be curled up in our laps when we would sit and watch TV. "Peachy-pie" was a lover. She was a loyal and kind dog. Her owner even certified Peaches as a therapy dog, and she went to nursing homes and visited with the elderly to keep them company.

Peaches was the opposite of everything the media has promoted about pit bulls. It was apparent by all who met her. She just wanted to be loved and love on people.

We also had another pit bull pet-sitting client named Rufus. He was a bit larger than Peaches, could really throw his weight (and slobber) around, but at the end of the day, he, too, was a loyal, loving dog. He would chase his ball and follow our commands. The rule of his house was that he slept on the floor at night, but he was always by the foot of your bed so he knew to escort you if you woke up in the middle of the night for a glass of water.

When we would take Rufus on walks, neighbors would be intimidated by his dark color and muscular build. It's too bad they didn't know that the minute he sat down his mouth would open wide to a large smile that would make anyone's bad day turn good.

Lawyers and Insurance Brokers are our Pit Bulls

If we don't protect our business, that decision could come back to bite our personal life. You don't want that to happen, right? Lawyers and insurance brokers are there to help you assess how much risk you are willing to take and to make sure that you are protected and understand that risk. They have lots of education under their belt and, most likely, a lot of experience. If they are industry specific, they might even be a terrific source of knowledge about potential hazards you haven't even thought of. They are there to protect you, and it is my hope that you embrace them. Don't be fearful of what they might tell you—or their bill! They are worth every penny.

The key to these relationships is for you to establish them before you need them. You want a lawyer and an insurance broker you can trust and call, knowing that they will respond to you when you have a crisis after hours. They really can be the biggest asset in your company. Just like the pit bull, they might seem scary, but, in reality, they are there, like Peaches, to curl up on your lap and give you kisses.

Unfortunately, most of us only speak to them after the initial establishment of our business—or when we are in trouble (gulp!) Let's take a closer look at what each of these team members can do for you.

Lawyers

Lawyer pit bulls are necessary for every single business. They may appear intimidating, but a good lawyer will be loyal and there to walk you to the kitchen to get a drink of water at night (well, not really, but you know what I mean!). They will ask you the right questions to understand your motivation for your business and your long-term goals. They will foresee liabilities before they occur and help you understand how to mitigate the damage or avoid it from happening.

Lawyers have gone through years of schooling to pass the bar exam, and they specialize in many different areas of expertise. Businesses might need a lawyer to help with contracts, employment agreements, copyright infringement, or getting a trademark approved for your company. There are so many instances that can come up that the initial connection of a great business lawyer can help tremendously down the line.

I have known some business owners who needed a lawyer after a client threatened to sue them or had an employee who wanted to question their practices. If the person didn't have a lawyer they already worked with, they had to scramble at the last minute to find one.

Sometimes a new client might question the contract that the business owner downloaded from a website online. The business owner doesn't know what to do because they falsely thought that since it sounded legal that it was good enough. This type of ignorance could really leave a business open for major liability! Always have a lawyer review your contracts.

Although I am most certainly not a lawyer, I see a lot of contracts that don't address the protocol for a conflict. Is it arbitration, mediation, or do you go straight to court having to defend yourself and pay the lawyer fees? A good contract would have this in place. This is important because most small businesses don't have the funds to shell out tens of thousands of dollars to lawyer up and protect themselves. In many states you can actually add these mediation and arbitration clauses, so, at the first sign of conflict, it doesn't put the business in a monetary disadvantage by having to go to court.

Unfortunately, some business owners would rather go to a Facebook group and ask their friends for legal advice than face their fear of what an actual lawyer would say, along with the bill. Don't be fearful. They will not bite you. They will lick your face! Okay, well not really!

Remember! This can really come back to bite you down the line.

Case Study - Aubrey

I had a consulting client, Aubrey, who loved to do everything on her own. When she first began her business, she would copy other contracts that she would find on the internet, slap her business name on them, and start having them signed by her clients. She even did this with her employee handbook. She copied it from another pet sitter she met through a Facebook group, who got it from another pet sitter, who said it was lawyer reviewed.

I always chuckle when someone says, "it is lawyer reviewed" because different states have different laws. It is always important that a lawyer in your state, with knowledge about your company, reviews your documents.

Aubrey presented this employee handbook (legal document) to her staff and had each one sign the last page, acknowledging all the policies and procedures of her company. Then one day, unexpectedly, one of her employees, Taylor, quit. She didn't even give two-weeks notice.

Aubrey was shocked and caught off guard. Taylor was great at her work and never gave any indication that she was unhappy. More so, she didn't even give Aubrey a reason why she was leaving. Aubrey felt betrayed and hung out to dry.

Eventually a few months went by and Mrs. Caddy, a long-time client of Aubrey's called. After Taylor left Aubrey's company, Mrs. Caddy stopped booking. She had a Goldendoodle named Xavier. He was like a giant stuffed teddy bear. He was a great dog, and Mrs. Caddy always wanted him walked at 1:00 pm Monday through Friday. Aubrey was happy to hear from her as she was a $125 a week consistent client.

"Hi, ummm Aubrey? This is Mrs. Caddy. Remember me? I am Xavier's Mom."

"Oh Hi Mrs. Caddy! How are you? I haven't heard from you in a while. We have missed you! How can I help you today?" said Aubrey.

"Well, umm..." Mrs. Caddy sounded awfully nervous on the phone. "Aubrey, I haven't booked for a while because I have been using Taylor. I knew she left your company, but Xavier just loved her so much that I didn't want to change sitters on him, so I accepted Taylor's offer when she asked me to stay with her. Oh gosh, I am so embarrassed now."

Aubrey couldn't believe what she was hearing. How could Taylor solicit Aubrey's hard-earned clients? How dare she! Admittedly, Aubrey was upset but held back and listened to Mrs. Caddy.

Mrs. Caddy continued, "Aubrey, Taylor didn't show up for two visits. I just don't know what is going on with her. I don't trust her anymore, and I really want to hire you back. Would you have me back please?"

We all know that Aubrey welcomed her back with open arms, took her booking, and now had a client for life. Mrs. Caddy had a new respect for the way Aubrey ran her business. She realized that working with a company with a business owner who was involved in the daily operations was a trust that she couldn't get many places. Mrs. Caddy wanted to know that Xavier was always taken care of and she knew that Aubrey would make sure it happened.

It was a year later when Aubrey told me this story, and she was still infuriated. So, being her business coach, I asked her, "Did you have a lawyer review your handbook?"

Sheepishly, Aubrey replied, "No, I copied something that one of my pet-sitting friends posted in our Facebook group. I thought it looked professional and didn't even think to have it reviewed. She said it was looked over by a lawyer already. I trusted it."

"Aubrey, how long did Mrs. Caddy not book with you?" I asked.

Aubrey replied, "About three months."

"Aubrey! That was, potentially, $1,500.00 in lost revenue because your former employee was never aware that she wasn't legally able to take your clients with her. Granted, just having that in writing might not have eliminated this from happening, but getting a lawyer on your side to show you where your document has loop holes in it might have instilled enough fear that Taylor might have thought twice about taking your clients with her."

And personally, I wondered how many others.

It was then that Aubrey finally realized that her fear of paying a lawyer to review one of the most important documents of her company would have been money well spent because it might have made Taylor think twice about taking clients from Aubrey's company.

Lawyers are there to predict and prevent horrible things from happening in the future.

Aubrey was furious about the lost revenue and the betrayal

she felt from Taylor. So, Aubrey did go to the lawyer and was advised that the only recourse she had was the option to send a cease and desist letter. Aubrey was advised that, typically, this was a scare tactic because following through with it would cost Aubrey a lot of time and money for it to come to justice. Plus, the damage would have already been done. It is really hard to prove that in court.

The moral of Aubrey's story is to have a lawyer on board in the beginning of your business to make sure that you are set up for success and to protect yourself! I would almost call this protection love for your business which is just like Rufus and Peaches. Business owners need to be diligent. They need to know the people who know employment laws, and that the wording of their service agreement will hold up in a court of law.

The risk can be outstanding, even put a small business out of business if they don't have the proper protection and loyalty looking out for them as they navigate through the night to grab a glass of water as Rufus did.

Case Study – Char

I have a private Facebook group online where members post questions about challenges they are currently experiencing in their business. I remember this one time when my client, Char, posted that she wanted to enforce her cancellation policy. She told the client she was keeping her money because she canceled at a moment's notice. She wanted to charge the client $500.00.

Although, rightfully so, the client pushed back saying that she never signed anything to that effect and challenged Char to take her to court. She knew that Char didn't have the resources to sue the client.

There are so many instances where you need to make sure that you are protected and when things are contested, you have a trusted advisor, whom you already have a relationship with that you can call upon for answers…or backup!

Another pit bull a business owner should hire is an insurance broker.

Liability Insurance Broker

When you start a business, you will need business liability insurance. As the business owner, it's important to have advisors who will help you understand what to do if something happens.

Having a personal insurance broker that you can always call upon and get solid advice when accidents happen is crucial to the outcome of any situation. Every business owner should know their insurance agent. Even have their number on speed dial.

There are two major types of insurance they will help you with:

1. *Liability Insurance: If something happens to your client's property.*
2. *Workman's Compensation Insurance: If something happens to your employees*

Having an insurance broker who will answer your questions endlessly is key. When your company expands to bringing on staff, they can help you understand the protection that you will need in the way of workman's compensation. I've known them to advise companies on best practices to mitigate the possibility of putting in claims. They can be a wealth of knowledge, if you let them.

To illustrate the unpredictable nature of this a pet-sitting business, here are a few mishaps that have happened in my coaching community:

1. *During a meet and greet to a new client a dog jumped up and bit the pet sitter on the face.*
2. *A sitter was walking a large dog on a leash and was pulled down to the ground when the dog saw an off-leash dog and took off. She ended up with a broken nose and plenty of bruises, but since she hit her head*

when she fell, they did a lot of costly scans at the ER to be safe.
3. An employee was riding a motor scooter between jobs, hit a pothole, went flying off the bike, and suffered a traumatic brain injury. Currently tally $50K
4. A dog walker walking a dog on the snow slipped and fell on ice. She fractured her fibula and hurt her knee. She was out for four months and workman's compensation paid all the bills and her lost wages.

I am sure all of these business owners didn't start off their business thinking, "what if this happens?" But each one had a trusted insurance broker that they could call. Can you imagine trying to deal with that all on your own? Can you imagine trying to call into a 1-800 number and trying to get the information you need to help work your case?

This discussion pertains to any industry. The situations will vary, but the need to have a plan and a team in place is paramount.

Your business insurance agent/broker is there to be your buddy. Allow them access to your business and decisions to help guide you through the process and coach you about what you could expect. Let them explain your options. They will help you eliminate the fear by educating you on the proper ways to protect your business.

Of course, every business owner hopes they don't need to utilize their insurance or their agent, but it sure gives you peace of mind when you know who to call to get accurate advice.

Here are some reasons I often reach out to mine:

1. I want to have an event and wonder if my insurance extends to another location?
2. I am attending an event and they need proof of insurance. Can you send me something?
3. A dog chewed up a couch and the client wants me to pay for it. Do I have to?

4. A pet sitter slipped off the last step on the staircase and can't walk. What do I do?
5. A sitter, who was bitten by a dog, wonders how she is going to pay her bills while healing?
6. What does my coverage cover? I can't understand the book that the insurance company sent me!
7. What happens when X happens?
8. Should I file a claim?
9. Who do I call when X happens?

There are so many questions I have had to ask over the years. My insurance agent has always been there, not only to answer my questions but anticipate the questions that I didn't even know I had.

Now that is valuable.

David Pearsall is an insurance broker with Business Insurers of the Carolinas. He has become a great friend of mine and we have done many interviews together. I asked David if he had a case study to share with you that would illustrate just how important having a relationship with an insurance broker can be to your business.

David had this story about Sam to share:

Case Study – Sam

To illustrate the importance of having insurance, let's look at the following case study:

Sam opened up his pet business, Sam's Pet Sitting and Dog Walking, LLC in 2010. The first couple of years he purchased liability insurance and bonding, then in 2013 he felt like he was paying for nothing, so he dropped his insurance coverage entirely. In 2015, Sam's business really began to take off and he hired five more employees to assist with all the new clients. Sam still had no liability or bonding coverage and neglected to purchase workers compensation insurance to cover his employees for injuries they might sustain while working for his business. At the end of 2016,

Sam's business grossed over $500,000 in revenue, and Sam was on top of the world! And then, THE CLAIM occurred.

On Friday, March 13th, 2017, Sam got a call from his employee, Maria. Maria was obviously shaken up, as she was crying and breathing heavily. She let him know she was walking a client's chow chow at the park when it began barking at another dog l being walked by a couple of teenagers. All of a sudden, the other dog pulled away from the teenager's grip and charged at them. Maria attempted to get between the two dogs and was knocked down and bitten multiple times on both hands/arms and shoulder areas. Then a gentleman biking in the park stopped and tried to assist her in breaking up the fight by using his bike as a shield. He, too was bitten. The dogs finally stopped, and the teenagers got a hold of their dog's leash and left the park. Unfortunately, Maria, the client's chow chow, and the bicyclist were all in need of medical treatment for their injuries, and Maria was looking to Sam for direction.

In the days and weeks that followed, Sam's life began to spiral. First came the call from the client. Their chow chow accumulated a vet bill of $8,700 to repair its left eye, which was damaged by the other dog. Because they could not locate the teenagers or the dog that caused the injuries, they were looking to Sam to pay the bill. Sam was initially hesitant to pay, but after speaking to his attorney he came up with the $8,700 and paid the client.

Maria's bites were severe, so much so that she lost feeling in all of her fingers on her right hand. She required surgery, and, to this day, is still unable to hold a utensil in her right hand. Her medical bills have exceeded $20,000, and she still needs another surgery. Initially Sam said he would pay for her treatment, but after paying the first doctor bill, he told her he could not afford to pay anymore at the current time. Maria, devastated, reached out to a workers' compensation attorney, who advised her to turn the business in to the state's Office of Workers' Compensation, and proceed with a lawsuit. The state's Office of Workers' Compensation came in and fined Sam $100 per day for every day he did not carry a workers' compensation policy. Since he met the legal requirement for carrying the coverage back in 2015, the fine amounted to $73,000 (a workers' compensation policy would have only cost his business $3,000 a year). Maria's lawsuit is still pending, with a current demand on the table for $500,000. Sam has hired an attorney but has been told he has no chance of winning.

Last, the nice gentleman that came to Maria's aid during the attack also reached out to Sam to pay his medical bills, as he received twenty-four stitches for a gash in his right forearm. Needless to say, Sam was out of money and had no insurance. The man filed suit and currently has a demand for $100,000 to cover his injuries and lost time from work. Again, Sam's attorney advised there was very little chance he will get out for less than $50,000 on this liability claim. Sam's attorney then asked him what it would have cost to buy liability and workers comp insurance for his pet-sitting business. Needless to say, Sam is no longer in business, however, the suits are all still pending.

Don't Let Fear Creep In

Dealing with contracts, legal issues, and insurance (accident) issues are often highly charged emotional situations that can leave us paralyzed with fear, unable to make a wise decision.

In the previous case study, one could say Sam was scared of spending too much on insurance or wasn't scared enough. Others could be scared about the sheer cost of having a contract created, they are scared to say the wrong thing to an insurance agent and have it used against them. They are scared that their staff will do something wrong to bring on more liability to the business. I have heard hundreds of fears over the years and most of them are not based in fact.

Don't be afraid of protecting your assets. Find the right insurance agent who really understands your industry, so they can think ahead and protect you from the liabilities that you might not even be aware of. This is big my friends.

How do I find my Pit Bulls?

Finding a Good Lawyer

Start by seeing if there are any popular business lawyers in any local networking groups you attend. If not, ask business owner friends you might have in the area. If that doesn't work, there must be a small business that you use in your city that you can ask the owner who they use. Moral of this story, ask around! These days, just a simple post on social media can go a long way. Look for a business lawyer.

When you are interviewing them:

1. Ask them why they are the best choice.
2. Ask them how long they have been doing business in your industry.
3. Take notice of how long it takes to get a response from them and how much time they spent not only answering your questions but trying to educate you on the entire process.

Finding an Insurance Broker

Most industries have associations that are connected to some insurance companies. Your best bet would be to start there to find the insurance agency that can be there to protect you.

When you interview them:

1. Ask them why they are the best choice.
2. Ask them how long they have been doing business in your industry.
3. Take notice of how long it takes to get a response from them and how much time they spent not only answering your questions but trying to educate you on the entire process.

Trust me, you will want to have a couple of pit bulls that you can call on when there is a pile of doo-doo that needs to be cleaned up. You'll be glad it is a relationship that you have already cultivated knowing they will be there to help you discern the facts and take the fear out of the equation.

Homework

1. Make sure all of your contracts (including employment) have been reviewed by a lawyer.
2. Ask your lawyer to review your employee handbook and employee applications.
3. Ask your insurance broker to review your liability policy and tell you where you are open for liability.
4. Ask your insurance broker to shop a better rate for the same or better coverage.
5. Talk to your insurance broker about workman's compensation and discuss at length all that is involved in your company. Have them help you brainstorm about things you could be doing differently to protect your workers.
6. Learn about the workman's compensation class codes and how it is determined in your state. Know everything you can.

3
THE BORDER COLLIE: SYSTEMS AND PROCESSES

If you have ever seen the agility of a Border Collie, you will agree that it is simply amazing. They are smart, fast, and full of energy. Border Collies are working and herding dogs that love to focus on their tasks. In fact, they work best when they have a job or a process to follow. They react very well to commands and follow directions. If you start telling them the beginning of a task, they will tell you the end by completing it. They are highly intelligent and very excitable.

Max and Mia

Max and Mia, two black-and-white border collies from the same litter, were an incredible team. They operated as one. They had a strong herding streak in them, and when we let them out for their lunch time exercise, they would be a machine!

Here is how it would happen:

The minute we went out in the backyard they ran to the pillar where we kept their tennis balls. Just staring up at it. Jumping a little and barking. As if to say, *What are you waiting for? Get the ball, human!*

One of us would throw the ball across the yard, and Max would run the full length while Mia would go halfway. She would cheer him on by barking while she waited. Max would retrieve the ball and drop it in front of Mia. Then, she would pick it up and, together, they would happily run back to me and present the ball at my feet.

They were obsessed with this routine.

They would do this routine in the pool. In the living room. It didn't matter where they were, this process would not stop. They had this laser focus and wouldn't deviate from the plan. Because of it, they were fast, efficient, and had same result every time.

Why You Need Border Collies

Systems and processes help build a business's brand. They give your customers a feeling of consistency. Your customers want to know what to expect. After all, that is why people return their business to you again-and-again. It gives them peace of mind. Or it can have an adverse effect, but, for the sake of this book I will go with the positive!

Border Collies are the employees who run your day to day operations. They include the office manager and field managers. They are the employees who implement and ensure that everything you need to make the business run smoothly goes well. They enforce the rules and initiate the processes of things, like schedules and check-ins. Systems and processes can help avoid this from happening and help rectify it in a habitual and non-emotional way when it does.

An effective office manager maintains the business flow. Tasks will vary from business to business, but they can control the employee's schedule, the bookings from clients, payments received from clients, billing, customer service, and a plethora of other things.

The supervisors make sure that the staff is doing what your manuals instruct so that the clients will always have the same experience no matter who they interact with. Supervisors also act as a good representative of the company to keep employees engaged and educated.

Case Study – Hotel Branding

When you stay at a Marriott, Hyatt, or Four Seasons you can expect each brand to deliver the same scripted experience. One gives you warm cookies when you check in. Another always has fruit water in the lobby. It doesn't matter if you are in Houston or Boston, the experience is going to be the same because the brand has built in systems and processes. From another, you will expect top notch service and welcoming front desk attendants, bell hops, and room service. You know they are out to impress you and always be courteous. These companies have designed their brands in a specific way and the supervisors make sure the processes keep going so the guest always has the same experience.

Another super example, is McDonald's. I once took a trip to Munich, Germany and you know what? A Big Mac and Egg McMuffin taste the same exact way in Germany as they do in the USA! I knew I could rely on the brand to be consistent and give me something familiar in an unfamiliar environment.

These systems and processes are like powerful Border Collies that can show up in many areas of your business.

Using systems and processes to your advantage:

Perhaps things in your company are exceptionally amazing. Did you know that you can condition your customers to always have exceptional experiences through doing all the right things?

Imagine if you never lost one client due to lack of systems and processes? What if your systems never failed, and your clients only left for other reasons beyond your control? How much business revenue could you retain by having incredible systems and processes?

I would argue that if your customers knew you were normally "on the ball" that they would be willing to let a few mistakes go because they know how hard you work and how reliable you are.

Unfortunately, it doesn't always go that way.

Without a few border collies in your business, bad things can happen. How many times have we heard of people getting retribution online via blogs, reviews, writing a letter to the CEO, tweeting, or even writing blogs about their experience? I bet that these business owners didn't have a system or process to give their customer a bad experience, but it happened. In Hug Your Haters, written by Jay Baer, he says that most upset customers just want to feel like they are being heard.

Let's take a look at what can happen if your systems fail and your customer doesn't feel like they are being heard.

Case Study - Mary Jo

Mary Jo was an angry customer and destruction ensued. Mary Jo didn't get the experience she was looking for from the company she hired. She called on Friday and was told she that a manager would call her back to help. When she didn't hear from the manager on Saturday, she called back. Again, she explained her problems and was promised that a manager would call her. Trying not to be the bad guy, Mary Jo gave them one more chance and called again on Sunday after she didn't get a call back. Not only did Mary Jo feel upset that her expectations weren't met, but now she had an entirely new, and more frustrating, problem. They weren't calling her back. She fired off an angry email to the company via their website and then went to the internet to blast the company on every major review site on which she could find them listed. Mary Jo just wanted to be heard and feel like someone cared.

The company very easily could have avoided all of this. Who knows what the actual problem was? Did the message not get to the manger? Did the manager not have instructions to call back angry customers right away? Did the customer service person who answered the phone not have enough power to help Mary Jo at the moment she needed something? Whatever the culprit, the system failed Mary Jo and the company. Mary got her retribution by telling the world of her terrible experience and the company lost out on winning back an angry customer for life.

If you own a business right now, take heed of this story. At some point, whether you intend to or not, you will have a Mary Jo calling you. You must plan the right things to say and do in order to take someone who is angry and make them a customer for life. How you deal with a mistake after it is made will make or break any company. Having a system or procedure in place will mean all the difference in the world to your employees and to your customers.

That will lead to your happiness :)

When receiving a bad review, it is important to remember that you are responding to the public as well as this one person. You want to appear professional and leave the impression that you are approachable, reasonable, open to concerns, and solution oriented so they can know what to expect (there is that word again) if they ever have another dispute with your company. So, do it with humility and honesty.

When You're Caught Between the Customer and your Staff

There is nothing more nerve-wracking than when a customer has a complaint about the services your company provided. Even more so, when it is an employee who caused the upset. We wonder, *Did the worker really do that bad of a job?* We feel in the dark, helpless, upset – basically, a lot of emotions! We want to get to the bottom of it, but sometimes it is tough to determine the truth.

We find ourselves in the middle.

We don't want to tell the client they are wrong, and we don't want to falsely accuse our staff, but we do want to investigate so it never happens again. It could be the case of a bad worker, poor expectations, unreasonable client, misunderstanding—many things!

Here are three steps you can add to your process of how to handle these complaints. Keep in mind each business will be slightly different.

1. You need to view the process as a fact-finding mission. You are an investigator. Investigators reserve judgment until they listen to both parties. This can be on the phone, or if you can, in person. It is important to not blame anyone. Ask open-ended questions. Do not accept any responsibility and validate their feelings.

"I understand you feel..."

"So, what I understand is..."

"Can you tell me what the desired outcome for you would be?" or *"How can I make this right?"*

Once you have received all the information, let the person you are speaking with know when they can hear back from you. Giving them an expectation is important in this conflict resolution.

2. Repeat step one with your employee adjusting it to them. Be aware of your tone. If they did mess up, I always love saying, "I understand why you did it this way this time, but in the future can you . . ." Or you can retrain them on the parts of the manual they didn't follow correctly.

If it appears they didn't do anything wrong, it is important not to talk bad about the client but let the worker know they did a good job and you have their back. It will allow for open communication in the future and make them feel like they can trust you. It will solve the "I didn't want to tell you because . . ."

3. Follow through on your promise to get back in touch with both parties with a resolution.

In the end, our customers buy from us because we are solving a problem for them. They must remain confident that we can continue to solve problems. Whether it is the problem they come to us with or another one that develops. That is why they trust our company enough to buy from us.

How strong are the systems and processes in your business?

Could you hire someone today who could walk in, read your operations manual, and do exactly what you want them to do?

The best way to see if your business has a Max and Mia is to try to step out of it. Step out of your business for a few days and see if it still runs the same way. Any business that you want to scale, should be able to operate without you in it.

Sure, there is some element of "no one will be me" but can you remove yourself or replace yourself like Marriott, Starbucks, and McDonald's all can do? They have trained their Border Collies to work the processes, and, because of it, I can go to Germany and have the same experience as in the USA.

Training and conditioning is key.

Max and Mia didn't just learn this all overnight. They were trained and conditioned to do so. They have repeated it thousands of times. How can you do this in your business?

Systems Checklist

1. Manuals
Are the systems and processes all written out?
2. Employees
Develop a training program for new hires so they all learn the same information in the same way. It is important to give every member of your business the same opportunity to excel in their positions. They need to know the rules of the game, and those rules need to be documented so everyone can do it the same way.
3. Payroll
Develop a process for staff to submit payroll and pay them on time.

4. Brand Ambassador

Every employee is a brand ambassador. Develop a hiring process. During training, each employee should learn how your company works and the why behind it. Develop scripts for them to use when speaking to customers on the phone and in person. Be sure to empower them in the decision making regarding customer needs, within reason. (Be sure to define "within reason"!) Be sure to support each employee when they ask questions or need advice.

By following your systems repeatedly, it will give you, your support team, and your staff the impression that there is direction in your company. They will want to perform well and "bring the ball back to you." It will give your staff confidence, empowerment, and let them know what to expect. This will make your life better because your staff retention will most likely increase.

Having these systems and processes will save you time and money. It will create efficiency, so you aren't always explaining or re-teaching things again-and-again.

Delegation

After you have worked out the proper systems and processes that work best for your business, it will be easier to delegate tasks to others.

You must be clear about what you want. If you aren't clear about how you want things to be delegated, a task that should take ten minutes could take sixty minutes. Most likely, it will create a lot of confusion and might even lead to frustration from the person working for you. They are looking towards you, the expert, to lead them in the right direction. Without clear instructions you can't delegate what you need to get done and that, my friends, is a big problem.

Some clients have said, "But Bella, I tried to delegate, and it didn't work out." I felt the same way when I first started. You know what happened? It got better because I learned how to give clearer instructions, ask the right questions, and choose the right people.

Tips to Delegate in an Effective Manner

1. *State your goal or objective.*
2. *Use as much factual details as possible.*
3. *Give a due date.*
4. *Give a priority level or due date.*
5. *Include pictures or links to examples if it is a creative delegation.*

So, you see it is vitally important to the longevity of your business to have Border Collies running around in your company. Without them your business would be a big tornado doing things over and over again.

Homework

Let's take you on a journey to see what you can get systematized in your company right now. Here are some examples to get you going today:

1. Do you have a foolproof process to let new clients sign up with your company?
2. Is your billing recurring or every day?
3. How are your employees scheduled?
4. Can your clients just schedule without you or do you need to spend time helping them sign up or pay someone else to do it? Side note: I see a lot of sales processes come to a screeching halt because the business owners make it almost impossible to keep the sales process flowing.
5. Is your marketing for new employees and clients on autopilot?
6. How do we follow up with clients after the sale?

7. How do we do quality control inside our own company?
8. What does initial and ongoing training look like?
9. What is the procedure for your social media accounts?
10. What content (blogs and videos) are you producing and at what frequency?

4

POODLE: NUMBERS AND ANALYTICS

What do you think of what you hear the word "poodle"? I am willing to bet it is something along the lines of refined, picky, prim, or proper? Am I right? They are, actually, the second most intelligent dog breed behind the Border Collie. They are known to be great duck hunters and water dogs but more recently, and for the purpose of this book, I am calling attention to the prestige and precision of how they must be cared for. Poodle cuts were originally created to help protect their joints, but coming from a pet sitter background, these pups require high upkeep and are often pretty particular. They have a double coat, which can often become tangled, which is why regular grooming needs to happen.

Our CPAs, bookkeepers, and website developers are our poodles. Everything in these areas needs to be specifically cared for and requires a high intelligence to execute.

Valentine

Valentine was a very prim and proper poodle. When Nicole, from Miami Pet Care, would go to visit her, her owners always had specified particulars to follow. Nicole recalls, "Valentine was definitely too smart for her own good. In her youth, Valentine would decide when she didn't like something and, from then on out, she wouldn't do it. One example was that you had to lift her in and out of the car or on or off of the couch. No jumping for her. She doesn't like it."

Poodles are notorious for being picky. Their grooming requires precision, and even their hair is known to be good for those who are allergic. It is hypoallergenic, proving that they are just that much more of a special creature and particular at everything.

I once had a pet-sitting client with a poodle that would only drink reverse osmosis water from a certain bowl, near the refrigerator, with two ice cubes.

I kid you not.

Now before you say, "Bella, that is ridiculous!" let me tell you I tested that theory by taking out the ice cubes and changing the location of the water.

This poodle wasn't having it. So, whether it was the pet parent teaching and grooming for this behavior or not (hmmm...) the fact is still the same—this dog had a particular way of doing things. It had to be precise.

Why do we need poodles in our business?

Whether you want to realize it or not, your business is full of numbers. The CPA, bookkeeper, and website developer are just some of the experts that you need on your team to make sure the company stays properly groomed to perfection! There is no possible way that, as a business owner, you can oversee all of this long term. Not to mention that all of these areas are constantly changing. So, keeping up on the education, changes, and analyzing how they are affecting your business are three professions in itself.

Without knowing exactly what we are doing in our business or where we are headed, it just leads us to live for the day. This isn't bad in some cases, but we need a precise understanding of what is going on in our business and what it will take to get us to where we want to go. I would say that the larger concept is achieving your goals. How can you understand where you want to go if you don't know where you are? It would be like getting into a car in California and hoping to reach Boston without knowing what roads to take, how much gas you need, when to stop, where to rest overnight, and when you would arrive.

Business owners need specific knowledge about their business, so they can accurately forecast their projections. If this is neglected, the business owners often find themselves feeling burnt out and confused about what should be on their "to-do" list. I see it every day. Someone might say, "I want more dog walking clients," and I say, "Okay, are you a dog walking or pet sitting company?" and they say, "Well, I do both." I go on to advise them that they should pick one or the other to focus on and then run the numbers on what they need to get to where they want to be. Then, it needs to be reflected in everything, most importantly on their website. Knowing specifically what you want from your business will greatly impact every area of your business.

Certified Public Accountant (CPA)

This poodle will help you understand what is currently going on in your business (mostly on a yearly level) and how to strategize the best ways to achieve your goals. They are licensed by your state, aware of all the ever-changing tax laws, can do financial analysis for you, and ultimately save you thousands of dollars by implementing great tax strategies. Having to switch CPAs each year leaves a business exposed to not having someone vested in your company long term, so it is important to find someone you like and make them feel like they are a part of your success!

Bookkeeper

These are the people you will become very close with. They will often take care of everything in your business that deals with the day/weekly/or monthly numbers. This could be a variety of things such as:

Accounts payable:

- Pay your bills in a timely manner
- Record payments from checks/credit card receipts according to type
- Reconcile your bank statements to your company books
- Reconcile your credit cards/vendor statements to company books
- Collect W-9 forms from vendors as needed
- Prepare/distribute vendor 1099's at year end
- Transmit 1099 copies/summary to IRS at year end

Accounts Receivable:

- Bill your clients for service
- Collect/apply payments to client accounts
- Charge client credit cards for services
- Prepare monthly statements for clients
- Make bank deposits

Payroll:

- Collect/retain all required federal/state tax forms
- Collect/retain employee time sheets for processing
- Calculate payroll expense by employee
- Calculate employee tax withholdings and employer tax liability
- Print payroll checks or make direct deposits
- Make timely tax deposits to tax authorities

- Prepare payroll registers summarizing payroll expenses and taxes
- Record payroll and tax expenses in financial records
- File quarterly tax reports to federal/state/local authorities
- Reconcile monthly and quarterly payroll expenses to quarterly tax reports
- Prepare/distribute year end W-2's to employees

Independent Contractors:

- Obtain/retain W-9 forms from contractors
- Receive billing statements of services provided in time period
- Review statement for accuracy/compliance with terms of agreement
- Pay contractor for services
- Prepare/distribute 1099's at year end as for all vendors

Cash Management

- Prepare cash flow projection based on scheduled payments/receipts
- Notify owner of cash balance and short-term cash requirements as needed
- Transfer or advise owner to transfer funds to/from checking/savings as needed

As a business grows, bookkeeping is only the beginning of the what a business owner should know.

Website Developer

People often mistake the website developer for the person who makes the website look pretty. That is not the case. This is the person that builds the website and makes sure the doors and windows work. A developer will make sure that your site is speedy, attractive to Google, responsive, looks good on mobile, will help with updates, and install any plugins you might need. It is very precise work and one wrong move could put a major kink in your website. Since most of us rely heavily on our website making our business look good, it is very important to have someone like this available when you need.

Case Study - The Old Bella

When I first started out in business, I used to think that I could just print out my statements at the end of the year and categorize them myself. Part of this was that I didn't realize what a bookkeeper could do, and the other part was I was afraid of spending more money.

But after the second year of sitting down with a bottle of wine (okay it was two) and all my bank statements and credit card statements printed out trying to categorize an entire year of expenses and income, I was over it and knew I needed help.

What I realized is that I was doing myself a disservice by trying to do it on my own because I was not categorizing things in the proper place. I knew I spent cash on some things ten months ago and never recorded it. I even wondered if everyone gave me the checks they owed me or if there was anything outstanding? I was a hot mess to say the least. It hurts to think about how much money I probably lost simply because I wasn't accounting for every single penny. Who had time? I was too busy wearing all the other hats in my business!

In fact, when I finally did relinquish control, I was made aware of just how much money I was "forgetting" to collect and realized how many checks I "forgot" to deposit. They would get lost, shoved to the bottom of my purse, and more. Then there were expenses that I wasn't even recording, so, essentially, I was claiming that I made more money than I did and not taking all the deductions I was allowed because I didn't keep correct track of anything. That realization hurt me to the core, and I vowed to never do that again.

Another advantage I enjoyed once I employed a bookkeeper was knowing the pulse of my business. Was I spending too much? Could I pay myself more? Was it possible to hit new goals because I understood where I was at financially and where I was headed? It gave me so much power! It made me feel like a "real" business owner who could make decisions based on the numbers. I felt accomplished knowing what all my hard work meant to the bottom line of the business, and I started a competition with myself to keep outdoing myself each month. It revived my excitement for my business!

The realization that the CPA and the bookkeeper do very different jobs was eye opening. Let me tell you what I mean.

A CPA is like a sand castle builder while your bookkeeper is the one who provides the plastic sand castle molds, shovels, and buckets to work with. When you go to your CPA once a year, they can only build a sand castle with what you give to them. This means they can only do your taxes with the information that your books give to them. They are not responsible for going through receipts and accounting for each penny. They are there to take your year-end statements and plug them into a calculation to tell you what you owe in taxes. Just think, if you made $100K and you had $40k in expenses vs $10K in expenses, it would make a big difference. What would that do to your bottom line? If your tax rate was 15% (rough estimate) that could be the difference between $9K or $13,500 owed in taxes. Big difference, right?

Case Study - Erika Godwin, The Barketing Blog

Erika is an incredible marketer and website developer. She is one of the most knowledgeable people when it comes to developing websites to make sure they are at their peak performance. I asked her to explain why this poodle is someone everyone needs and why it is hard to do it yourself.

This is what Erika had to say:

Is your pet business website performing?

Your website is your #1 salesperson. Therefore, it is vital that it be optimized and working for you, even when you are busy caring for pets or sleeping. A modern and attractive website is essential for first impressions, but it is also crucial that you do not sacrifice functionality over design. Your site should be collecting leads for you. Now, how do you know if your website is performing for you? Here are a few things to consider:

Mobile-Friendly

Poor user experience will damage your brand. If your website is not optimized for mobile devices, you will lose business with Google's new 'mobile first index.' Now, what does this mean? Well, Google will primarily be crawling the mobile version of your website before the desktop version to learn how it should be indexed for search engines. In a society where mobile device usage is increasing drastically, it is essential to make sure your visitors are quickly finding the information they are looking for. If it is not convenient and straightforward to navigate your site, prospects will go to your competitor.

Pro Tip: Add a button in the bottom corner of your mobile website to make contacting your business simple. Test your site with Google's Mobile-Friendly Test. (https://search.google.com/test/mobile-friendly)

Search Engine Optimization (SEO)

If you are not doing enough or ignoring your SEO, you are probably falling behind your competitors. Competition in the pet industry is high, and new companies are popping up every day. How do you stay at the top of the search results? If your SEO is a 'one and done strategy,' you will lose. You need to publish good content consistently. However, SEO alone won't guarantee success. If you rank #1 in Google, but your website is outdated, full of spelling and grammar issues, and is slow, you will lose those potential clients quickly.

Pro Tip: It is essential to do your research and use location-based, relevant keywords on each page of your website. A unique keyword or keyword phrase for each page is recommended. If you are using Wordpress, install the Yoast SEO Plugin. Yoast will help guide you through optimizing your content for search engines.

Call-to-Action (CTA)

It does not matter how much traffic your website generates if those visitors are not contacting your pet business. When a potential customer finds your website, you want to make sure it is easy for them to find the information they are looking for to increase conversions. Your CTA is the most critical part of your website for sales. It is crucial that the CTA on your homepage be above the fold and immediately grabs the attention of your visitors.

Pro Tip: Determine what your goal is for each page on your website and add one (1) clear and compelling call-to-action to each page. Keep it simple and to the point.

Google Analytics

Now that you have optimized your site for mobile devices, written SEO friendly copy and strategically placed your CTAs; it is time to start tracking your analytics. How many unique visitors are you attracting to your website? Where are they coming from? How many visitors are contacting your company? How many people leave your site after only viewing one page (Bounce Rate). This information is essential if you want a website that performs. Dan Zarrella says it best, "Marketing without data is like driving with your eyes closed." Data should be an integral part of your website strategy. It will tell you to what is working, and what isn't so you can make the appropriate decisions to grow your pet business.

Pro Tip: It is important to understand how your prospects find you. Sign up for a free Google Analytics accounts and add the tracking code to your website. If you are not tech savvy, try adding a Google Analytics Dashboard plugin to your website to have access to necessary analytics details.

Speed and Load Time

Your website may be full of beautiful images and fancy features, but the longer they take to load, the more likely your visitors will bounce. All images on your website should be compressed, not just resized. When you resize an image, you are downloading the entire image on the web page before it displays, thus slowing down your website.

Pro Tip: Test the speed of your website using Pingdom. Pingdom will give your website a performance grade and insights on resources to help you improve your website speed and performance.

(https://tools.pingdom.com)

Your website is working for you 24/7. Set your website up for success just like you would train an employee to ensure they are productive. Your website will be the first impression many potential customers have of your pet business. Make it a good one!

Let's Talk About Facebook Advertising

Facebook advertising is the number one way you can find your exact target market. Facebook is the largest database in the world. The best part is you can tweak the campaigns to create the best results. But you either need to know how or have a poodle on your team to keep up with this sort of thing.

Here is an example: You don't just turn the water on and jump into the shower, do you?

You test the water. Let it warm up. Then when it is optimal temperature you jump in the shower, right?

Facebook ads are just like that. Not only that but this "shower" is so smart it can create data and remember the exact temperature, spray feature, and height that you liked so you can make sure to have more precisely awesome showers to come.

Sounds silly huh? But it is true! If you are like me, you have no idea how to operate this highly complex shower so before hiring someone to help you program it all, you might just jump in a cold shower, shiver the entire way through, and then jump out moaning and groaning that you can't stand this shower.

Well, my friends, you need poodles in your business. Find them. They are out there. Once you do, you will start loving your showers! You will also start loving it when you have a steady flow of potential clients and employees applying to work with you!

So many numbers!

The poodles in your employ will help you plan the services in your business because they are the analytical, statistical, and trending numbers type of people. They will help you decide how to invest money, if what you are doing is working, and how to be so laser sharp in your focus that you can't possibly go wrong. There will be a lot of testing, correcting, and continuing but unless you have a bird's eye view of what is happening, you may simply find yourself running around in circles.

I find that the businesses that have a great pricing structure are able to afford themselves the choices to make to great things happen. It is true that money makes the world go around, so if you are wondering which dog you need the most, I would encourage you to hire some poodles. Without a bookkeeper and CPA advising you on the one thing most business owners hate (numbers), you might never get any traction.

Homework

1. Ask your network for referrals for any of these professionals you need on your team.
2. Set a date that you will have hired them and engaged their services.
3. Find a bookkeeper.
4. Have a tax planning session with a CPA.
5. Find a web developer to develop and monitor your site.
6. Decide if Facebook advertising is going to be a part of your marketing plan.
7. Learn about Google analytics and set it up.
8. Define your fiscal goals and what you need to do to achieve them.

5

JACK RUSSELL TERRIER: MARKETING AND PROMOTIONS

A Jack Russell is, typically, a small, brown and white dog with a LOT of energy. They love stimulation and are lively and entertaining. Always the life of the party, they are constantly bringing everyone together. Jack Russells are quick, intelligent, and do not like to be bored. They are the perfect breed to help illustrate the talents needed in your marketing and promotions departments.

Millie

Millie was a three-year-old Jack Russell. She would literally run circles while walking forward! It was a talent. She would always be smiling—you know how dogs smile right? They open their mouth real wide with this glowing happy light beaming out of their eyes? Her stubby tail was always wiggling, and the minute you sat down, she would jump on your lap and lick your face. When she was done, she would nuzzle up against you as if she was hugging you.

The minute you thought, "Ok, we will cuddle," she would jump back up, bathe your face in more licks, do some more circles on the couch, and then plop on your lap, belly up and bum wiggling. She was saying, "rub my belly!"

Millie was FULL of energy, always making you smile and always the life of the party. Hardly ever did she lay down and leave you alone. She loved to play with her squeaky toys, would want to impress you for treats or scrap pieces of food, and was always in the same room as you. Basically, she was the "happiness police" and the center of attention!

Everyone needs a Millie in their company. Without a Millie, your business would be in trouble.

Why You Need A Jack Russell

In order to attract people to your business, you need to have positive energy, lots of time, and the ability to get them excited and fall in love with your brand. Chances are this can't happen while you are getting pulled in so many different directions and exhausted all of the time because you are wearing too many hats.

It takes time and creativity to be the Jack Russell. You must be outgoing and engaging at community events where you are able to get people to interact with your brand and want to hire you. You have to be soothing and inviting when at networking meetings to build your connections in the community and get to know other business owners so you can build mutually beneficial relationships. Once you have staff, it is in your best interest to keep them engaged and excited to be working for you and representing your brand, but often we aren't sure how to motivate them or even how to stay in touch with how our staff is doing. Being a Jack Russell can be exhausting.

In any business, the Jack Russell is the marketing and promotions department. She is the energetic one with the outgoing personality. She loves talking to people at community events where you may have a booth or go on Facebook Live to help promote the story of your company each day.

The Jack Russells in Your Company

Marketing person: this is the person with the ability to talk to anyone that would represent you at events with a booth and promotional items. It is the person who would attend networking events, make connections in the community, and open the doors for opportunity to collaborate with other business owners.

Human resources consultant: This person advises you on ways to build staff morale. They can help you understand what motivates people, how to attract the right employees, and how to keep the people you love on your staff. Sometimes this task is harder than the dating scene, but this person is usually an outgoing, people person, always seeking a happy outcome. You need this person.

Case Study - Susan

Susan was very analytical. She liked to analyze numbers and look over spreadsheets. She liked to make lists and make sure everything was perfect. When the phone rang, or a customer walked in the door of her business, she would freeze. She would hope they wouldn't speak to her because she was shy. She tried to put all the information that a customer would need online and expect them to read and know everything from what she presented. After all, she would analyze someone's website so why wouldn't everyone do that with hers?

But she was very wrong. Although she was incredible at her craft, she severely lacked the skills that Millie the Jack Russell has, and, because of that, potential clients would lose interest because there wasn't any excitement around her brand. The entry to do business with her company was cold so she would lose the people who needed that extra love, touch, and warm and fuzzy. It was through that warm and fuzzy that people gain the confidence to press that purchase button.

Have you ever been shopping and researching a product online, debating if you should get it? You convince yourself you want it, put it in your cart, and then click away from your cart never to return? Somehow, the website didn't give you the excitement to actually finish the purchase. This is so important for companies to learn how to do, either virtually or in person.

Events in the community

When asked to do events in the community, Susan had the most professionally looking booth. Her table cloth was ironed. Her business cards were neatly stacked. She had free promotional items lined up on her table, and she had on a clean work shirt with her branding. Her hair was done, her makeup was perfect, and she even wore perfume. She stood behind her table and waited for people to approach her to ask her about her business.

But nothing she did stood out.

Susan thought events were failures. They were not a good investment of her time and money spent to participate. In her eyes, she wasn't seeing the return on her investment (ROI). Susan defined ROI as gaining new clients either at the event or shortly afterwards.

The Millies of the world would have had a totally different approach. They would have put the table towards the back of the space and would have stood out front. They might not have the most ironed tablecloth, but they would have some sort of interactive activity closest to where the foot traffic was passing by. A Millie would have engaged with the crowd, asking them questions, drawing them in. Her ROI would include the ability to capture leads to work at a later time through phone numbers, emails, or addresses. Perhaps even through getting them to click onto the company's Facebook Page. Millie would have understood that the event was a way to *start* a relationship, not get to third base or hit a home run!

Here is a list of things that a Millie would take charge of:

1. Hiring Staff

Every business needs to hire talented people to work for them. Without talented employees, we can't scale our business or achieve what we originally set out to accomplish in the business world.

Have you ever taken inventory of how much your employee is worth to your business? How much more could you do with employees? How much more money your business could make? How much more productive you could be? How much more you could scale your business?

Putting it into the perspective that you want to have more staff because it will get you closer to your "WHY"... is powerful. If you can see that the potential new hire in front of you is worth forty thousand dollars of revenue in your business, then your interviewing style might take a turn for the better. You might start to hone in on your interviewing skills and improve your training methods.

The Millies of the world are great at hiring! They know how to market the business to attract the right type of person that the company is looking for. They are charming and inviting during interviews, and they are a terrific brand ambassador, in case you haven't noticed already.

The Susans of the world have a tougher time with hiring. They often give into the stinking thinking of the world when they have trouble finding good workers. They might say, "it must be my location" or "if I offer more pay, maybe I will find the right person."

I call this mad marketing with stinking thinking.

Susan needs a Millie in her company to go flop in people's laps and say, "rub my belly" and make them laugh. She needs a person who can be outgoing, engaging, endearing, and connect with people in a way that isn't uptight and dry.

We all need a Millie in our business in order to thrive and keep our pipeline flowing with customers and workers. Without a Millie on your lap, the pipeline will dry up, and you could become that business owner who is constantly looking for customers or staff.

It is the reason why some businesses claim they have too much business or can't hire fast enough, and others say that they can't find enough clients. Once you get going and establish a recurring system where you can continuously feed your business with customers and staff, it will be smooth sailing.

2. Sales

Most people I speak with hate the word "sales". They don't like to be sold to, and they don't like to sell. They think it is a slimy word, and they don't like to be rejected.

But guess what? If you don't sell, you will not have a business. You need to learn how to sell in a manner that you are confident about. An unconfident seller won't sell anything.

There is a saying that you need to be able to sell ice to Eskimos. This is what one company, Ship Foliage, has done. If I said to you, let's gather five maple tree leaves, some maple syrup, and one ounce of candy and ship it around the world, would you think I was crazy? Many would. But the person who had the courage to do this is selling this package for $49.99 a box and is making a lot of money doing it. The same person, will also ship you actual New England snow. Their site is called www.shipsnowyo.com and they will ship snow from New England to any location.

Ship Foliage was not afraid to sell. They were not afraid of rejection. In fact, I would say that they embraced the word "no" and refused to listen to their friends and family who probably laughed at them when they told them what they were going to do. I don't know them personally, but I would venture to guess that they have a bit of Jack Russell in their breed!

3. Branding

When most people think of branding, they think of the colors and design of their logo. But, really, a brand is that intangible feeling that lives in the hearts and heads of those you do business with.

You don't dictate what your brand is. Those who do business with you do.

For example, we all know Nike. Nike's message is to "Just Do It." They are trying to encourage people to stop being lazy and get up and do whatever it is that they need to do. They are making people feel as if conquering a big challenge is just as simple as "Just Do It" They have inspired athletes to get up and practice. To get that basketball through the hoop. To get up and take action.

Amazon, is trying to show people that they can cover just about anything from A to Z as the arrow in their logo shows and make you think of them for anything you need, fast, and at your doorstep. I think every Mom who has had a baby at home and used Amazon Prime to get diapers delivered to her front door can attest to this. The Moms feel like Amazon is their own personal girl Friday bringing anything they need in a click of a button. They feel supported because Amazon seems to have everything!

Brand management is rarely addressed in small businesses. It is easy to understand because as small business owners, we have many hats to wear. Although, if there is a negative view about our company, or even worse, no view about our company out there, how will we be able to grow? How will we able to be memorable in the hearts and minds of our potential customers and woo them over enough to hand us their credit cards?

It is important that we have someone in our company helping maintain the brand, someone to make sure our presentation at events is reflective of how we want our patrons to feel. It is important that we are able to present our customers with the same feelings each time they have interactions with the company.

Think about Disney for a moment. I bet your inner child just smiled, am I right?

How people feel about your company is going to be the difference between them trusting you enough to keep paying you for your services or being easily wooed away by the next sparkly business that tries to distract them.

4. Networking

Do you like to be out and about? Do you enjoy striking up a conversation with a stranger? Getting to know people in a business networking setting? Or do these situations make you shudder?

Networking is a necessary evil. Most traditional networking happens during three types of settings. Knowing what makes you most comfortable will help you choose a setting where you can be most successful.

Morning networking meetings are what I like to call, quick and dirty. Everyone there has to get off to work, so everyone is there for a purpose. Everyone sits at a table, and the meetings are structured with specific start and end times.

Afternoon networking events are typical lunch and learn where there is a presenter, attendees are seated, and food is served. It is a lot more low key and knowledge and relationship based.

Evening networking events tend to be larger with many people. Typically, drinks are served and the end time is open. Since it is after work for most people, there are no elevator pitches. Usually, it is just a mob of people chatting it up!

Each type of networking event has a life of its own and each attracts different types of people. There seems to be a group for everyone, you just need to look hard enough to find it. Almost every industry has some sort of networking group. There are also faith-based networking groups, women's groups, men's groups, mom's groups, multi-level marketing groups, and so much more.

The question is, can you find the one right for you?

Goals of Networking Groups

The number one thing I hear from those who have gone to networking groups are, "Bella, it was a waste of time." When I investigate further as to why they say this, they mention that they didn't get any clients from the event, and people just tried to push their cards onto them.

Now let's take a step back folks.

This isn't what networking is about. Networking is about building connections to start a relationship with someone. Speaking from personal experiences, here are just some of the benefits I have received from networking:

- Free training on topics I otherwise wouldn't have gotten.
- Connections to a new building opening up in my town that became a strategic partner for my business.
- The ability to get to know key people I would end up hiring for my business, like a lawyer and CPA.
- The opportunity to become "known" in the community resulting in producing the largest pet fashion show that Scottsdale, AZ ever saw on a high fashion runway at the Barrett Jackson Car Show!

Networking is only a way to start weaving your brand into the community. It is like any other relationship in life. What you put into it is what you will get out of it.

Here's a tip: If networking still gives you the heebie jeebies, why not contact the event organizer and see if you can volunteer to help? What better way to meet people than to have a job helping. You bet that organizer will do everything they can to help increase your exposure and connections because you are helping them when they need it the most. These events aren't always easy to pull off.

All four of these vital skills require someone with a little bit of Jack Russell. Someone who isn't concerned with upsetting people. Someone who is all about spreading the love, running around, having fun, making people smile, making customers feel so good that they become friends and keep coming back.

These are major components that every single business needs

especially when they want to grow or scale their business. Most of the time a Jack Russell is exactly what a business needs when they have plateaued.

Homework

Think about your business right now, what can you be doing to be a better Jack Russell?

1. Are there places you can look for staff that you have never tried before?
2. What are two or three events that you can commit to having your company represented at this year?
3. What networking groups are going on in your area that you can make a commitment to attend at least twice a month?
4. Call three HR companies and see what problems they can help you solve.
5. Hire an outgoing sales person who will bring in more sales by networking and attending community events.

Do this for three to six months and see what types of opportunities this new consistency provides you. I have a feeling it will be bountiful! (From personal experience, of course!)

6

BEING A BUSINESS OWNER IS TOUGH!

Now that we have covered the basics, let's sit down and have a little heart-to-heart chat.

Being a business owner isn't for the weary. In order to grow a business, you must be diligent and intent on winning. You will need a team. Without one, a business can eat you alive. It is my wish that you, the incredible business owner who just spent the time reading this book, take a serious look at how you can structure your business for the utmost success. No one else has the dreams and goals that you have, and no one else can get you there but yourself and your decisions.

Here are a few final thoughts, a pep talk that you can review from time to time if you are feeling lost or confused.

Consistency will be key!

The toughest lesson about consistency is that it takes FOREVER to see the results. You just need to keep chipping away, and, eventually, you will get to where you are going. You can't stop. You shouldn't stop. You have to be so strongly connected to your

"WHY" that when you get knocked down you jump back up faster saying, "You won't knock me down the same way again!"

Failure isn't bad.

Did you know that your relationship with failure and self-doubt will determine your destiny? I see it all the time. Those who acknowledge that failure is a part of life, that they will fail more than they succeed, are the ones that ultimately get to their goals. Successful people decide to learn from their failures; it is about the journey to their goal. Once you get to your goal, then what? You make another goal! So, if we spend the most time meandering towards our goals, we might as well enjoy the ride.

The dog park might feel chaotic but everyone there has a job to do, and, together, it creates that wonderful fun place. You need all of the dogs there to play together and get along. With just one dog, it really isn't that much of a dog park. You need different breeds of dogs all having fun to have the entire concept succeed as a whole. Just as dogs, all of us are different breeds. Some of us are really great at sales and marketing while others are great number crunchers. Sometimes it is so hard to get out of our own head enough to even know what we are really good at doing, so, in the end, I believe the question comes down to: which, of all the business tasks needed are the ones that you want to do?

You will kiss many frogs before you find Prince Charming.

Do you know how many CPAs I have had over the sixteen years I have been in business? Too many for me to remember. I have also had more web developers than I can count. Your needs might change, relationships might die out, sometimes your contractor might just go AWOL. But what I want to you keep in mind is that you must keep a great network of people around you because once you find someone, it doesn't mean they are with you forever. Don't get discouraged if the relationship doesn't work out. Don't adopt the mindset that "I can't find anyone that will work as hard as I will" or "I can't find anyone." You have to stay positive and keep looking. Don't let the failure of trying to find the right person discourage you from finding the right person (or dog).

When you find these incredible people for your team, establish a procedures manual so that each time they are doing something great, you can add to that manual. Simply ask them, "Can you add step-by-step of what you are doing for X project in the manual please?" Granted, some dogs like the poodle can't do this for you. However, when it comes to networking, sales, running credit cards, and promotions, there are processes that you can write down so the next dog that comes into your pack can see exactly what is needed. This works wonders! It is about working smarter, not harder. This will help you eliminate having to re-explain how to do things or even understand how things are being done.

Here is a personal example. Feel free to steal!

Even though I like to try to insert a coupon code myself via my WordPress website, for some reason when I do it, it never works. So, I asked my developer to create a coupon for me and then provide me with the step-by-step instructions, with a screen shot, so I can do it the next time. You know what? The next time I tried it myself, it worked! I can also send the instructions to my assistant and have her do it if I am too busy. These simple things typically make your contractors happy as well, because these are simple tasks that you could do yourself. The money you spend with them can be used for the major tech things that are just over your head.

Think about when you dated people. You had to kiss a lot of frogs before you found Prince Charming, right? You didn't stop at the first horrible date, did you? Finding people for your team is going to be a lot like that experience. The strong don't just survive, they thrive. No one can do it all on their own. Think of the most successful people out there. Sir Richard Branson has a team. All the sharks on *Shark Tank* have teams.

Don't try to control everything.

You have to be able to let go of the control and allow people to help you. You have to embrace the process of making mistakes and choosing the wrong people, so that you can find success with the right people. Personally, by having the right team on my side in 2017, I was able to increase my company by 241%! There is no way that I could have done everything on my own. Everyone needs these dogs in their business and only you will decide if you actually can find them or not.

Be the leader of your business.

Your dogs will need direction. Learning how to delegate is paramount to your success. If you can't accurately and precisely explain what your expectations are and what tasks you need help with, then they will not be able to deliver. In essence, I have learned that you usually get back exactly what you asked for. Tell the contractor what you need and give them the due date you would like. Before you hire them, find out if those expectations are realistic. Or, if it is a larger project, you can say work until $X or X hours and then let's see what you have done. That is a great way to not run up your bill and have sticker shock in the end.

Be the leader of your life.

All that we have learned here really starts and ends with one's own self. A business owner needs to be self-reflecting to see what they really want out of life and out of their business. A big advantage to having all these dogs playing together nicely is so you can have the opportunity to be free enough to do what you want. Perhaps that is building an empire? Perhaps that is just putting it on autopilot, so you can receive regular paychecks. Or perhaps, it is so you can go and snuggle with your children at home, take them to and from school and add to your family's future financial security.

Whatever your "WHY" comes back to, it is you, my friend, who is the only person who decides if your business fails or survives.

Create your pack and be the leader!

7
TAKE THE QUIZ: WHICH DOG ARE YOU?

Take the test! Which dog breed are you? This is meant to be a fun, non-scientific test that you can take to see which breed you score the highest in. By no means is it a clinical diagnosis but meant to get you to think about what dog you are least like so you can work on trying to find that dog to add to your dog park!

Circle the one that best describes you with the pair then tally up how many you circled for each letter:

A _____ B _____ C _____ D _____

D. Everything has its spot, and I don't like anything out of place.
C. I thrive when I know what to expect and what to do.

A. I love accounting for every penny in my business.
B. I love being the life of the party.

C. I like to write down steps and directions.
A. I enjoy tracking trends and statistics.

B. I can easily talk to strangers.
A. I spend a lot of time looking at Google analytics.

A. Tax code is exciting to me.
D. I color within the lines, never outside.

B. I understand people very well.
D. I only see black and white, no gray.

C. I like to read the instructions when starting something new.
B. I don't mind speaking in front of others.

D. I like to take things apart to see how they can be put back together.
A. I do well with numbers.

C. I would rather someone tell me what to do than figure it out for myself.
D. I like to plan things out and not figure out as I go.

A. I like to study and stay up on my states legal statues.
C. I achieve a lot of my goals.

B. I see it as a personal challenge to sell someone on a product or service.
D. I love numbers and finding trends in spreadsheets.

B. I feel like my life is an organized chaos.
A. I like to be able to project what is going to happen.

B. I base my decisions on how I feel when making business decisions.
D. I find the challenge of math to be fun.

D. I am very analytical when it comes to breaking tasks down step-by-step.
C. I am good at breaking down the steps to solve a problem.

C. I am good at explaining how to do things in detail.
B. I have a creative mind and eye.

D. I like to have a plan for everything.
A. I believe in right and wrong. There is no middle.

A = Pitbull
B= Jack Russell
C= Border Collie
D= Poodle

RESOURCES

National Association of Bookkeepers
http://certifiedpublicbookkeeper.org/

National Association of State Boards of Accountancy
https://nasba.org/

SCORE office https://www.score.org/

Jump Consulting www.JumpConsulting.net

Personality tests 16 personalities
https://www.16personalities.com/free-personality-test

Barketing Solutions http://barketing.co/

Business Insurers of the Carolinas
https://www.business-insurers.com/

Hug Your Haters, Jay Baer
http://www.jaybaer.com/hug-your-haters/

ABOUT THE AUTHOR

Bella Vasta resides in Phoenix, AZ with her husband Alex, daughter Olivia, and rescue mix, Rocco the Rockstar. She is a graduate of Arizona State University with a BA in Human Communication. In 2002 she began a pet sitting company which went on to be nationally and locally award winning until she successfully sold it in 2016. In 2007 she began Jump Consulting, a consulting company focusing on helping dog walking and pet sitting businesses start or expand and has grown that into a popular blog, podcast, Youtube channel, and speaking career. She also has written for Entrepreneur magazine and been featured in Huffington Post amongst many others. Her motto is, "Always Keep Jumping."

www.ingramcontent.com/pod-product-compliance
Lightning Source LLC
Chambersburg PA
CBHW031542210526
45464CB00003B/1107